Just Like Being There

Just Like Being There

By

Frank Davis

ISBN 1-58721-204-8

1stbooks – rev. 3/15/00

A special thanks to *Gene Gould*
who's comment about my poetry,
hence the name
"Just like being there"

To all my friends and groups
who attended my poetry readings,
encouraging me to write this collection.

Thank You!!

I dedicate this book to
my wife **Donna,** *who is my biggest fan*

INDEX

PREFACE

IN 1986 Frank Davis wrote his first poem. His thoughts were of our attitudes toward the Indians and how we Infringed on their territories and lives.Most movies depict the Indian as bad and we were lead to believe they were our enemies. After reading more realistic books gave him a different view. In many Instances the Indians were friendly and helped pioneers In stress.

In two of his poems he brings out his own version of their real struggles of the Invasion of the white man, to be out numbered and controlled In a no win situation.

Then his thoughts of his childhood and memories of growing up, his slant on life and visions in a folklore atmosphere. His love and feelings of life and mother nature, to read his poetry will aquaint us with the Inner person and will remind us of our selves in many ways.

His first twenty poems were recorded and a friend listened to that first tape and exclaimed " Frank" its just like being there, hence the name" JUST LIKE BEING THERE".

In 1993 he married his best friend and was Inspired to try writing lyrics to show his true colors to her.She is his biggest fan and finally some one to add rhythm to his life. Maybe some time in the future, one or two of his lyrics
will be put to music.

JUST LIKE BEING THERE

GOOD TIMES

MEMORIES & YARNS

FOLKLORE &HUMOR

COWBOY POETRY

IMIGRANT TRAIL

PERSPECTIVES

NATURE

WHAT'S IN A POEM

A poem helps us to see
A poem helps us to hear
Helps us appreciate
Makes our visions clear

It answers questions
Clears up ones thoughts
Gives proper perspective
Lets us call the shots

Poems have honest meanings
Bring depth to our views
Lets us be ourselves
To say what ever we choose

To open up ones mind
Take the mysteries from our souls
We each are one of a kind
Sets a pattern for our goals

A rythm to our notions
Our sense of direction
Brings out our hostilities
Or shows our affection

Lets us speak our mind
Without pressing for attention
Our views are available
Our thoughts are in suspension

The spirit In a poem
Brings together a bond
It gets our attention
Lets us think beyond

1

A poem Is a bonus
A spirit with wings
A vision of our memories
Of people, places and things

A poem tells the story
Takes away the complications
Tells It how It Is
Simplifies our explanations

The mysteries of a poem
Are a delightful recall
A meld of understanding
That touches us all

PATH THAT I DREAMED OF

Our paths are like a road map
Seems Imposible to meet
That special kind of lady
That has rhythm to my beat

My dream was finally answered
She happened to be In line
With the path that I had dreamed of
And let me call her mine

I'm down off my high horse
And down from that cloud
I'm so very fond of you
I did my self up proud

I'll always love you dearly
With my feet back on the ground
You changed my frowns to smiles
And turned my life around

FINALLY

Some times we look a life time
For a special lady to meet
We just keep on looking
Never except defeat

I looked the whole world over
Thinking what shall I do
Then I attended a party
Thats when I found you

You were sittin by a window
And paying me no mind
I came by and spoke to you
You answered me In kind

I paused when you returned my smile
Sat down and asked your name
You helped me pass the time
And friends we then became

Oh you are so beautiful
I love you oh so much
Your eyes and lips so pretty
So sensious to touch

Now that I finally found you
never more will I roam
Lets you and I get married
With love that builds a home

ONE IN A MILLION

When life shows Its miseries
And I travel that lonesome road
Like carrying lots of burdens
With a tired team and a heavy load

I'm looking for a detour
To hide and think out loud
To gather my senses and self esteem
To do my self up proud

I've weathered the storms of yesterday
The worst of them I've seen
As I look out over the fence
The grass Is realy green

I jumped that fence and never looked back
The farther I went, the greener It got
I left those storms behind me
Looking for a rainbow with a pot

I sat at the end of the rainbow
Looking for a friend to meet
I found a lovely princess
Got up and gave her my seat

I felt like I was having a dream
She gave me a thank you smile
You look lonely and I am too
Why dont you sit a while

We saw a lot of each other
Since that rainbow went away
But the colors still are with us
Since that special day

You know, theres a better life out there
If you take the right detour
You,ll find some one to love and care
And greet you at the door

I'been loved and pampered and taken care of
Spoiling me to the nth degree
I'll do my best to return that love
And she'll take care of me

Donna, you're my sunshine on this earth
You're what I've been looking for
I'll love you for all I'm worth
For greeting me at the door

NEWLY WEDS

Remember, the love of your life
Has to be number one
To share all ups and downs
And share In all the fun

To understand the future
Always remember what you've got
To understand each other
To give It your best shot

Share your love and tenderness
Where ever you may go
Be kind and considerate
And help each other grow

WE CAN TELL YOU'RE IN LOVE

We can tell when you're in love
Cause your face Is all a glow
Your attitude Is happy
Body movements to and frow

You move lighter on your feet
And have no time for books
Your step Is a lighter beat
And more careful of your looks

Yes we can tell when you're In love
Cause your face Is all a glow
Your attitude Is happy
Body movements to and fro

Your time Is back on schedule
Your face Is all a glow
It's Impossible to hide ,that
You have finally found your bo

BEAUTY BEYWEEN THE EARS

When looking for a soul mate
To share the waning years
Dont over look the beauty
The beauty between the ears

They may be cute and sexy
Competing with their peers
Dont over look the beauty
The beauty between the ears

I finally found my soul mate
Over came my mental fears
I really saw beauty
The beauty between the ears

To find the Inner beauty
One goes by what he hears
You've got to hear the beauty
The beauty between the ears

IT SURE DID ADDLE MY BRAIN

I've never been kicked by a horse
And never been hit by a train
I sure was hit by the love bug
It sure did addle my brain

We were both looking for someone
Someone who really cared
Someone to believe in each other
And have true love to be shared

My brain still seem's to be addled
And we still are sharing our lust
It's easy to be true to each other
When you find someone you can trust

Our love overtime has been proven
The love bug still addles our brain
We never let go of the love bug
Tho our lives may be on the wane

I've never been kicked by a horse
And never been hit by a train
I sure was hit by the love bug
It sure did addle my brain

16

FAMILY

I might just be your brother-in-law
And I don't have an axe to grind
But since I married your sister
I'll tell you whats on my mind

The love between me and your sister
Is as strong as it can be
I'm proud to be your brother-in-law
And be part of your family

I'm proud that you excepted me
Excepted me for who I am
Your friendship means the most to me
Because I know you give a damn

I'll always be good to your sister
And be a brother to you guys too
Lets never break that friendship
We'll keep it, whatever we do

SHIVEREE

I don't have to worry
About your love for me
It couldn't be any better
Since our shiveree

Shiverees used to be popular
The noise and revery
To celebrate our wedding day
And you sat on my knee

To quiet the noisy crowd
You passed out candy bars
While I greeted all the guys
And passed out big cigars

We left on our honeymoon
With tin cans tied to the car
Toilet tissue streamers
But we didn't get too far

We were stopped by a patrolman
We were making too much noise
I explained to the officer
Mischief from the boys

He told us about the laws
He told us about the bans
Now here is your ticket
Better untie those cans

Don't leave them in the road
Don't leave us all your junk
No where to leave the cans
He said, put them in the trunk

The trunk is loaded with gifts
We are on our honeymoon
No way to start our marriage
To get in trouble so soon

Now since you both are newly weds
I'll void the ticket for noise
For this little joke was planned
It was ordered by the boys

Ten years of marital bliss
Still laughing about the noise
That started off our honeymoon
That officer and the boys

TO MY DAUGHTER INLAW "CAROL"

A jewell is to be cherished
A jewell is to be enjoyed
A moulding of a friendship
Sometimes to fill a void

A jewell has a special meaning
Like a person with lots of poise
To show a lot of charisma
Without making alot of noise

It takes a special being
To fit that kind of mold
To show that special nature
Another chapter to unfold

My daughter in-law is that special person
Not a diamond in the rough
But a jewell that is polished
And finished just enough

It took my son to find her
He found this four leaf clover
Could never find one kinder
If he'd looked the whole world over

I extend my love and friendship
It's so easy to be your friend
I hope you'll always be there
And our friendship will never end

TO A SPECIAL LITTLE GIRL "DANIELLE"

Its every grandfathers wish
To have a granddaughter like you
To have, to hold and to be proud
Of everything you do

I hope when you grow older
To be a grand parent like me
To have a grandchild to love
And plant a special tree

Your tree is growing pretty
It gives us a special bond
Its beauty reminds me of you
To whom I'm very fond

So when your growing up
And life looks sort of vain
Think of that special tree
Bucking the cold, the wind and rain

Always remember your grandpa
He planted that tree for you
And as it gets grown and pretty
You will be beautiful too

HAPPY BIRTH DAY, DEAR MOTHER

You remember when
I was just a little boy
Every now and then
I would bring you joy

It was easy to love you
A love you didn't have to earn
Because a little boy's love
Was always your concern

You always looked after me
Took care of all my needs
You deserve my love
For all your special deeds

Your handicaps were many
In a tough world to complete
You gave me heck aplenty
For playing in the street

I remember how mad I would get
You would scold and I would fret
I knew who the boss was
And I knew what I would get

You would bring me in from playing
To do my usual chores
And I remember you saying
Do'em or don't go out of doors

You only said you'd spank me
If I got out of hand
You were the greatest mother
When I would take a stand

25

Your love controlled your patience
Sometimes I heard you scream
But when I was a good boy
You rewarded me with ice cream

I used to hang around the table
Watching you make pies
I'd sneak a pinch of goodies
You'd see me from the corner of your eyes

You'd chase me out of the house
And tell me to go shag flies
Back I'd come sneaking like a little mouse
I'd come to steal your pies

You used to take me fishin
With my bobber and my pole
We had a beautiful picnic
At our favorite fishing hole

I remember you heard a splash
A fish down by the dock
You ran to catch it in a flash
But I had thrown a rock

I didn't dare to tell you
You might get ticked off
And I didn't know what I do
I just stood there, I didn't even cough

We used to go to Grampa's place
And run around the woods
I'd swipe a bunch of cookies
And you'd catch me with the goods

But you always saw the good in me
And sometimes I was bad
I never wanted to hurt you
"Cause it would make you sad

One day when I was itchin
To swipe a loaf of bread
You caught me at my snitchin
With those two eyes in back your head

And if I acted sick
And played it real cool
You took action quick
And kept me home from school

The cruelest thing
You ever said
Stay home son
I'm putting you to bed

Mother, look
What you did to me
I was really ok
But you didn't see

My temperature was good
You wondered what was wrong
But I was feeling better
When I heard the school bell gong

I'd better stop now, Mother
Before you get mad
I was only kidding
The best friend I ever had

With all my love, Happy Birthday

OPEN MIKE

When I step up to the mike
When I start to read my stuff
All nervous and sweaty
I hope you like me enough

After a verse or two
My composure comes around
Block out the he be gee bee's
And I begin to settle down

I know when I take the mike
I'm being put to the test
When I over come the willies
I vow to do my best

So hang in there with me
Don't hasten to call my bluff
I'll try real hard to please you
I'm ready to show my stuff

GONE FISHIN

Sitting on the river bank
A watching my fishin line
There I sat a waitin
And the sun began to shine

Got to dreamin about a whopper
And drifted off to sleep
Leaned back aganist a tree
And my line began to creep

Saw that whopper in my dream
Prowling and on the lurk
Soon it hit my line
And I woke up with a jerk

Reel a screamin as it went
As I tighten up the drag
This lunker in my dream
Turned out to be a snag

I shook my head to clear the fog
Everything fuzzy and gray
Woke up in time to catch a log
But the whopper got away

FARMER BOY

He would see her every morning
At the first break of day
To repeat their ritual
Then be on his way

She was his one and only
He never let her down
She was always there to greet him
When he returned from town

She longed for their ritual
He caused her every whim
When she saw him coming
She went to be with him

They walked up the lane together
Under the moon and stars
They strolled to the gate together
For her he lifted the bars

She neither smiled nor thanked him
For indeed she knew not how
He was only a farmer boy
And she a Jersey cow

FRANKIE

I can't ever get caught up
I'm spinning my wheels a lot
It seems I'm in a rut
Soon my day is shot

I get up in time for coffee
But it takes an hour or two
To drink and read the paper
Half the morning I blew

Too late to start a project
Or finish a thing or two
The sun is up and getting hot
Its time for another brew

My afternoons are lazy
I'm always hanging crepe
I've taken so many breaks
I'm getting out of shape

The work will still be there
When tomorrow comes around
I'll just find a place to hide
Stay there till I'm found

If I didn't start these projects
I'd have more time to play
But if I don't get started soon
Its going to be hell to pay

Last night I turned in early
To try to rest my brain
Got up feeling chipper
Damned if it didn't rain

DON'T ASK HOW I'VE BEEN

Mother nature is my enemy
She tears at my seams
She scorches with sunshine
And her dampness rots my beams

My door's are tired and squeaky
My sides are caving in
Rafters are split and leaky
Don't ask me how I've been

Mother Nature don't have no pity
She don't give a darn
But I am old and gritty
I'm a rickety old barn

FIX A DENT

Having trouble with my teeth
Most everytime I ate
The commercial said Fix a dent
Would hold my upper plate

I bought a can of Fix a dent
At the local auto store
Tried it in my upper plate
I had never tried that before

The ad said get some fix a dent
Turns out I bought bondo
Bondo's made for fender's
How was I to know

Get your Fix a dent in a tube
Not a can from the auto store
That's why they call me boob
How was I to know

My teeth are permanent now
They again are part of me
The answer isn't Bondo
It was never meant to be

GRANDPA OF THE THIRTIES

Grandpa's up before the rooster
Just to hear him crow
Grandma's in the kitchen
Mixin up some dough

She's fixin to bake the biscuits
While grandpa does the chores
Milkin cows and gathering eggs
To sell to the stores

Grandpa's up before the rooster
Just to hear him crow
Grandma's in the kitchen
Mixin up some dough

Grandpa's a plain old country boy
A down home kind of guy
He eats when hes hungry
and drinks when he's dry

Grandma cooked on a wood burning stove
She read by a kerosene lamp
Did her sewing and knitting by hand
Patching holes for gramp's

His uniform is overalls
His shoes are hightop boots
A pair of gloves and an old straw hat
He wore Instead of suits

He minded his own business
Worked hard for his dough
Always up at day break
When the sun began to glow

To be a farmer in the thirties
Our memories of the time
Every thing going slow
Then it began to climb

Grandpa tilled the fields
Sweaty shirt and dripping brow
Worked with basic machinery
With a draft horse and a one bottom plow

Grandpa would'nt believe
The model A was here
To trade a horse and buggy
For a machine that looks so queer

You had to start it with a crank
Careful dont break your arm
It may be cute and funny
But it wont do on the farm

Grandpa laughed at the change of course
We cranked until we cried
Grandpa whistled for his horse
Then he'd prance with pride

Grandpa had an agenda
Did every thing according to hoyle
He had his feet on the ground
He kept in touch with the soil

Grandpa's up before the rooster
Just to hear him crow
Grandma's in the kitchen
Mixin up some dough

DANIELLE'S KITTY

My career of being Santa Claus
Ended by a three year old
She Identified my flaw
And she stopped me cold

After making my delivery
Changed my clothes and I returned
My grand daughter sat beside me
And she seemed real concerned

She snuggled up beside me
I didn't have a clue
She said, papa,Santa wears the same
Kind a boots you do

MY DAILY ROUTINE

As I get up this morning
Programmed to go to work
As I gather my senses
And the coffee begins to perk

The aroma of the coffee
Arouses my sleepy state
I synchronize the watches
To keep from being late

My mind begins to wonder
Whats in store for me today
The sun is on vacation
And the sky is dark and gray

There won't be any sunshine
It has to come from within
To start the day off right
And greet them with a grin

Rainy days are a blessing
To feed our daily needs
To perk up our enviroment
To sprout the tiny seeds

And when the storm is over
The sun will do its thing
Brighten up the greenery
And the birds begin to sing

It makes us look ahead
Put our worries on hold
Start the day off smiling
To find that pot of gold

I open the doors to go to work
First thing I hear is the phone
Answer it with a happy voice
Could be someone unknown

After a friendly chat
We settle in our daily chores
Sets the tone for our day
Soon as we open the doors

And as the day draws near
The sun settles in the west
We'd forgotten about the rain
And we're headin home to rest

Another day behind me
I hope it did some good
Twas nothing to brag about
I did the best I could

I thank my lord for helping me
He helped me thru the strain
Finished my day with sunshine
And thank you for the rain

FUN TIME REUNION

Have you ever stopped to think
Or even hazard a guess
We have lots of memories
Complete with a lot of b.s.

When ever we get together
Somethings we have to bleep
Be sure to wear your boots
Cause the b.s. gets so deep

We didn't get to finish
Cause now we're on our break
We'll take it up at another time
And laugh till our belly's ache

MY CAMPSITE ON THE RIVER

Across the Sacramento valley
To the sierra's in the hills
My camp site on the river
The answer to my ills

I dribbled my line in the ripples
To see if their biting yet
What an exciting moment
A battle I'll never forget

A trout jumped out of the water
As soon as I set the hook
That beautiful fighting fury
Just like it says in the book

I tried so hard to keep my cool
And prayed the line won't fail
Eighteen inches of rainbow
A dancing on its tail

It took my line and bowed my pole
As I tried to reel him in
A real fish story I had to prove
This fight I had to win

All that power on a six pound test
Took it deep into his hole
Rod still bowed and line real tight
Began to take its toll

Out he came for another pass
As I cranked as fast as I could
Danced some more and showed his class
The fight was getting good

Then it got tired and started to wilt
It's energy was almost spent
A sigh of relief and a feeling of guilt
I released the hook and away it went

MOTHER NATURE

Mother nature is only noticed
When she causes us alarm
She can show her temper
Or she can turn on her charm

She gives us a violent storm
And shows us bitter cold
Life takes a different form
Endless lessons for young and old

Mother nature shows her beauty
And a love that never stops
She comforts us and feeds us
With weather, goods and crops

If we use to much
And don't save the seed
Her balance will be out of touch
Theres a message we should heed

We must use it sparingly
She likes to reproduce
But if we use daringly
She'll say whats the use

Mother nature is my universe
I cherish her with my soul
To waste her good intentions
Will jeopardize her goal

Her resources are plenty
If we use them with respect
Be careful in our madness
It's our duty to protect

It seems we're only thinking
In our own selfish ways
Our resources will be sinking
And we can count our days

She is generous with her gift of wealth
We shouldn't tax her nerves
We should protect her health
Give her nourishment she so deserves

We must train our young ones
To respect and to behold
The gift of mother nature
It damaged we should scold

I'd like to make a motion
Mother nature lives forever
Use all of our devotion
Make that our endeaver

Our environment was left to us
A legacy in trust
Preserve our gift and pass it on
We owe it and we must

AWAKENING

When I awakened this morning
The air was supreme, and the sun was bright
I remembered a dream that I had last night

It was in the mountains
My outlook was bright
The rivers were fountains
That babble through the night

The birds were singing
and the falls were fantastic
My ears were ringing
This was not plastic

I study the trees
Their magestic size
Be careful the bees
They may be your demise

The branches will tell you
The age of a tree
And all of Its beauty
Is absorbed by me

The flowers are blooming
Their leaves are green
The most beautyful petals
That I've ever seen

The mountains and the trees
And the flowers and the bees
Are the beauty of nature
And every one agrees

Mother nature Is generous
With her penchant for growth
As I enjoy her beauty
I will take this oath

Protect mother nature
Dont damage her nerves
Give her the nurture
that she so deserves

MANS BEST FRIEND

A gift from mother nature
A prize that's really neat
Is a man and his dog
A friendship that cant be beat

Its never too demanding
The attention that it takes
Theres an honest understanding
And the partnership that it makes

A deep dedication
And a bond of trust
A fond admiration
A reassurance a must

The dog will always be there
His thoughts and his yearns
For that happy moment
That his master returns

He will run out to greet him
He'll dance and wag his tail
He wants his masters attention
Before he checks the mail

His master loves and pets him
On his way to the door
The master kisses the Mrs.
The dog is waiting for more

The dog will fetch the paper
Put it by his easy chair
Because he knows his master
Will soon be sitting there

After a final reunion
The master settles in his seat
And as he reads the paper
His dog is lying at his feet

The dog is trained to serve his master
Many feats that it employs
They work together hand in hand
And both of them enjoys

I'm talking about my neighbor
The bond between him and his dog
Their love for each other is no fluke
His name is Roger, and his dogs name is Duke

His dog is like a son to him
Their bond will never pierce
They have feelings for every whim
Their love is strong and fierce

Duke is always active
Drops a stick at roger's feet
Roger throws it high and far
Duke turns on the heat

Tears up the garden in a cloud of dust
Keeps his eye on the stick in flight
Roger's wife frowns in disgust
Roger hides his face in fright

Dukes tail is always waggin
His eyes are gleaming bright
It seems he's always braggin
He wont lose it from his sight

Roger's foreign duck caller
Turned out to be a fluke
He was only calling his dog
"Here Duke" "Here Duke"

TO STUDY AN ANT HILL

Have you ever stopped to think
Who you really are
You're a tiny speck
Like the mystery of a star

The earth is like a giant ant hill
We dwell in her outer shell
The earth is our cocoon
It gives us life in every cell

The forces that keep us moving
Like stirring the flavor in
A blend of continuity
Never to stop and never begin

The earth's battery is a magnet
Her blood is the water in her viens
Her body is the soil that gives us life
A constant churning that gives us rains

To study an ant hill
Duplicates our way of life
They ploy in constant harmony
Reproduce so as to survive

They follow a positive direction
A plan that seems to work
A never ending affection
A constant energy , never a quirk

Every one does their share
To make the end result
Will fight to protect their lair
From some other cult

57

The colonies are many
Their trails meet far and wide
They learn to work in unison
Mother nature is their guide

They seek out a location
To carry out their plan
That meets their qualifications
To feed and protect their clan

Ants dont have complications of ours
They dont have airplanes, bicycles or cars
Their world is quite simpler than ours
They dont have restaurants, schools or bars
But they have a keen intelligence
Their system is guided by different powers

Its almost like magic
The finesse that they use
A continuity that guides them
A spirit that gives them their cue's

Their habits are traits
That keeps them in line
They dont worry about drugs
Politics or wine

They are put here for a mission
We wonder what it is
They have ambition
Always in a hurry, always in a whiz

To keep the cycle going
To repeat in natures way
To honor mother nature
Tomorrow is another day

WAKE UP

Of all the people in the world
Theres only a few that earn their salt
As we notice in our daily ventures
We're out numbered to a fault

We used to dig a ditch
With our shovels and our picks
Now it takes an army
For the same amount of licks

Takes a backhoe and a loader
Two men to man the controls
A flag man and a superviser
For the same amount of goals

The machinery is worth a mint
And the wages are out of sight
To do a simple project
To waste all of that might

It costs a million dollars
To fix a normal task
To get an explanation
They question why we ask

The cost of a survey
Is more than the Installers
A simple two bit job
Can cost a thousand dollars

My vision of the future
Is a scary sight to see
We'll have to use a computer
We'll have to have a degree

We won't want to hustle
For we'll be out of shape
We won't have any muscle
No stronger than a grape

We'll all be useless beings
We'll be fat and on a diet
We'll litter the world with garbage
Then we'll all deny it

We won't have a need for beauty
Theres nothing to see in space
When we use up our resources
We'll find another place

We had better reconsider
Our position at this point in time
We should try to save the future
Or it won't be worth a dime

MY FATHERS SPIRIT

I wonder if he's here
He seems to be present
He seems to be near

He doesn't ask
He seems to know
He seems to be with me
Wherever I go

I try to make contact
But the connection is blurry
He seems to be there
And I shouldn't worry

I see him in dreams
His presence is there
He is always in touch
Never in despair

He hovers in my presence
I'm sure he is near me
I reach out to him
And I know he can hear me

He seems out of reach
But is ever so near
The feeling is strong
His voice I don't hear

I know he is with me
And feelings don't lie
He is not far away
He didn't say good-by

His journey was detoured
He went through a switch
I never could find him
I searched every stitch

Before his detour
He taught me some rules
He showed me his insight
He gave me the tools

To continue my journey
Go on with my life
Follow in his footsteps
Without any strife

Be loving and caring
And fight for what's right
Be it ever so precious
Whatever the plight

I follow his guidance
And share with my peers
He molded my character
In a very few years

I carry his message
Am proud to convey
His presence is with me
In whatever I say

My father is a spirit
And when I feel low
I think of my father
And get on with the show

Sometimes I wonder
Our learning is slow
Seems to be a mystery
What we really do know

We don't learn from words
Everything that we feel
There's that special magic
That makes our life real

If we slow down and think
On a wandering stroll
Our fondness and memories
Will unite our soul

I'll follow Pop's image
Carry on with my tasks
I'll always be ready
For my detour he asks

Even though he's on detour
He's on the right track
He knows I will find him
He need not come back

He has a one-way ticket
He's with his fraternity
I'm sure I will join him
For the rest of eternity

TO BE A KID AGAIN

They say to be a kid again
And attend the school of hard knocks
The need of an education
Instead of throwing rocks

Some kids are natural born losers
But most are on the right track
The ones that get into trouble
Seems they're running with the pack

Kids today think its hard
They want every thing under the moon
The world owes them for life
A life on a silver spoon

They don't try to understand
And they don't want to know
We had our share of hardships
Over fifty years ago

We didn't hear much radio
Or knew what t.v. was about
Didn't have a pit to hiss in
Or a window to throw it out

We made our own sling shots
Our arrows were sticks of weed
The squirrels were all on the ground
Cause all the cats were treed

We built our own go carts
As we did all of our toys
Always headin for trouble
For making too much noise

We wore cardboard in our britches
When ever our mom would say
Just wait till your dad comes home
we knew there'd be hell to pay

She knew how to keep us in line
We knew her word was our loss
We better damn well believe it
Cause dad was alway's the boss

We never messed with the old man
A razor strap was his tool
And anybody that crossed his path
Would have to be a damn fool

He knew how to harness our energy
He gave us lot's of chore's to do
They better be done when he got home
Or he'd spank our butts black and blue

Dad had no trouble with us
We had trouble with him
And if our work wasn't done
Our butts would be out on a limb

We had respect for our dad
His way was state of the art
He knew how to keep us in line
But you know we still loved that old fart

MEMORIES OF GROWING UP

I got into a lot of mischief
When I was growing up
Making noise and getting rough
They called me an ornery little pup

I could tell by the gleem in their eyes
They didn't judge me bad
It was just their surprise
I was going through a fad

I would watch their temper
And play my hunches cool
They were on to me
But I wasn't a fool

I knew when I had to mind
And didn't get so bold
They'd spat me on the behind
I'd frown and they would scold

And when I was a good boy
They would show their love
They were happy and proud
Of their gift from above

But then I had my off days
They wondered why they'd praise
That onery little rascal
Was going through a phase

They'd get down on their knees
And ask me to be good
If they said please
I promised that I would

67

If I was good they'd buy me things
Or take me to the park
Let me play on the swings
Sometimes until dark

They'd send me to the grocery store
To add to our lunch
The bottles would get broken
The cookies I would crunch

They'd bring me in from playing
To wash my dirty face
And it goes without saying
I was a hopeless case

Mom was doing the washing
And hangin out the clothes
I was jumpin on the bed
I fell and broke my nose

Mom really was disgusted
I threw pillows in the house
Her favorite lamp was busted
I was quiet as a mouse

She couldn't find the paddle
And she knew who did it
She was getting madder
Cause she knew that I had hid it

When I really amazed her
She sent me out to play
I threw corn cobs at the rooster
She brought me in to stay

She'd holler and she'd scream
And really get hoarse
She got crazy and she'd steam
I would change my coarse

We had a hostile neighbor
Said I'd wrecked her flowers
Mom took one look at me
And said, this kid isn,t ours

He just hangs around
He's not our kid
He's from another town
The neighbor blew her lid

The neighbor called the cop
He came knocking on our door
He said this has got to stop
Not to do it any more

I had to stay in the yard
And play with my toys
Being a good kid was hard
I couldn't even make noise

The days were long and lonely
My mom would get sad
She said she wouldn't own me
When I was really bad

And if I didn't mind
She'd have to tell my dad
That would get me thinking
I had really been had

To my pop I was good
He was tough and fair
I knew where I stood
He,d sit me in a chair

I knew I,d better sit there
Cause he meant what he said
And he didn,t care how long
Till I straightened out my head

My pop was always good to me
And of coarse he really should
But I knew his word was gospel
I knew where I stood

He gave me lots of lessons
He taught me the golden rule
He corrected my manners
Before I started to school

My pop was always proud of me
And I could feel his pride
But he was real finicky
His mind was cut and dried

SQUEAKY HINGE

I stepped outside one foggy morn
To a squeaky door hinge sound
I listened and waited, forlorn
You'll never guess what I found

The creaky squeaking sounded close
I couldn't believe my ears
A barn door squeaking do you suppose
Strange what someone hears

First I heard it in the north
And then it changed to south
The noise was going back and forth
I listened, stary eyed and gaping mouth

The freakiest thing I ever heard
Many hinges chiming in
A dozen doors swinging to and fro
A motion without any wind

The noise was getting closer
A strange feeling came over me
I couldn't tell where it was
What in the world could it be

Now I hear it over head
How surprises never cease
Strangest story you've ever read
From out of the fog, a flock of geese

PERSESPECTIVE

When we visit with our peers
Or deal with our clientele
As we while away the years
We seem to know each other well

Our meetings are casual moments
We follow the usual trend
Discuss the patterns of our times
Respect the closeness of a friend

We pass it off as normal
Our feelings are guided so
What ever the conversation
As if we didn't know

Our thoughts concern the moment
Projections of our times
Discuss the problems at hand
And our blood pressure climbs

When we get off by our selves
Our true nature comes to light
Our thinking is undesturbed
Its a good time to write

Try your hand at poetry
Your true feelings will unfold
You'll think of many experiences
Fantasies you've never told

Theres lots of pleasant memories
And fun things to think about
Put them down on paper
Gives your meaning a different route

It'll take you back in time
As your memories tend to unfold
Being surprised that you remember
It's yourself you've under sold

Always looking to the future
Makes it easy to forget
Theres a wealth of pleasant memories
We should hang on to them yet

Theres no rhyme or reason
To the happenings of today
If we use our old time values
Will guide us on our way

Take a moment to be a friend
We each can learn a lesson
Impatience has no end
It just keeps us guessin

IMAGE

While worrying about the world
And all the problems there in
To solve the problems and answers
You wonder where to begin

You need someone to listen
And stare you in the eye
One who believes in you
To be there when you cry

I found that special partner
Who doesn't give any sass
I found him this morning
He was there in my looking glass

He had always been there
Looking back at me
But I hadn't noticed
The features I didn't see

He promised me he'd smile
If I cheered up my act
Not to fret about troubles
Don't be so matter of fact

He'd help me to be happy
He'd share with my load
To check with him more often
The sincerity that he showed

To find someone who believe in me
Who would look me in the face
We could share our differences
Put our program into place

Our fears were not too complicated
We cut our problems in half
We could show our emotions
And it was easier to laugh

He put me on a schedule
He didn't cut me any slack
To see him every morning
To start me off on track

Start off with pleasant feelings
To cushion the bumps ahead
Remember your friend in the mirror
Have an easy day instead

I like the guy in the mirror
As I get to know him better
He strikes me as the answer
Of my feelings to the letter

You can find your own partner
He'll soften your frowns and brighten your grin
He'll give you back your confidence
Let you grow from within

When you look in the mirror today
Don't look at the outer reflection
Look into those eyes and feelings
You'll see the inner connection

Spend some time together
Share your feelings and think
He'll know your feeling better
When he returns your wink

Isn't it great to have a pal
To confide your feelings and notions
To work out the answers with someone
Who understands your emotions

Be good to the guy in the mirror
Cause he's a spittin Image
There'll never be one nearer
To back your line of scrimage

You'll never lose your love affair
No one can come between
You can always clear the air
So keep that mirror clean

40's   50's   & 60's

Looking back to yesteryear
Automobiles were a work of art
With their own personality
You could even tell them apart

They didn't have computers
But had Individual class
Now, styling is all the same
And production is enmass

Most times you could listen
And tell the model and make
The sound of gear's and exhaust
Or the sound of a squeaking brake

Since they've thrown away the mold'
You cant tell them apart
They all look the same
Without looking at the chart

We look down the highway
We see one, we've seen them all
No personal Identity
The classic's are standing tall

Even under the hood
They all look the same
Have no personallity
Guarentee's the classic's fame

MECHANIC'S ARE LIKE DOCTOR'S

When we fly an airplane
And the engine starts to balk
Its time to find a landing strip
We can't get out and walk

When our wheels are acting strange
And we drive into the shop
We put trust in our mechanic
When the gear's begin to pop

Engine dependability
Prop's, landing gear's and such
Mechanical fit and balance
Demand's special touch

A net work of systems
A partnership per say
Electronics and machinery
To keep them on their way

Keep the plane's in the air
And the car's on the road
Keep the ship's on the sea's
Perfection is the code

Mechanics are like doctors
Lawyer's and dentist's alike
They never cross our minds
When things are smooth along the pike

The many gear's in a drive train
Attached to a hundred part's
Repair manuels are his bible
With instruction's graph's and charts

His patience and his foritude
His ability to hide his stress
To take care of our problems
Work with feeling and finess

Engine's are like humans
The oil pump is the heart
The battery is the energy
For the computer to do its part

Remember, the humble mechanic
Learning's alway's on his mind
Want's to be your hero
To get you out of a bind

Like a doctor he check's the pressure
As a dentist, the teeth on the gear's
As a lawyer he check's the reason's
To abide by what he hear's

Like a surgeon that does the implants
Use's tools instead of a knife
To follow up and research
To insure a healthy life

Checks the record's chart's and graph's
He studies the status quo
With seminars and data
He's alway's in the know

Remember the lowly mechanics
They're always standing tall
They are your true professional
To be there when you call

PROFESSIONAL MYTH

Doctors lawyers and dentist's
Charge enormous fees
Claim to be professionals
And they give no guarentee's

Professioonal's call it practice
They charge for every call
Mechanic's have to guarentee
They have to be on the ball

Doctor's charge for second calls
Even for a common cold
Mechanic's stand behind their work
For everything thats sold

Mechanic's give an estimate
For every thing they do
Then comes the warrenty
And stand behind it too

It takes a true professional
To stand behind their work
We give estimate's and warrenties
And they take us for a jerk

Next time you see a doctor
And pay the office tab
The thing that they don't tell you
Theres another bill from the lab

The lawyer gets a retainer fee
To protect us from a sin
Put your money on the line
In case he doesn't win

Now who's your true professional
The one with a silent code
Or the one that stands behind his work
That keeps us on the road

A WINNING HAND

When we're dealt a hand of cards
We choose the ones we want to keep
Throw away the discards
Or play them all and weep

That's the way with friendships
We choose them from a heap
Throw away the discards
Or play them all and weep

We have to be a good friend
To expect one in return
Do unto others and
Then it will be their turn

Theres negatives among us
There'll always be a frown
Check out their troubles
Before you put them down

If they're just trouble makers
And make you a nervous wreck
Deal them from the bottom
Thats how to play this deck

Cotton to the positives
You'll deal a winning hand
Look for happy people and
A friendship with no demand

When you're with happy people
Show your brightest side
Everything will fall in place
At least you really tried

Some friendships are very subtle
Some are too far out
The ones with a sense of humor
Are usually a pretty good scout

Shuffle them card's and weep
Down and dirty is the game
Sort out all the bad one's
And have no one to blame

Good luck now and play the game
Keep your eye's and ears alert
Go for the winning hand
Watch out, don't loose your shirt

DON'T SHOW YOUR MAN THE DOOR

Don't show your man the door
Till you've got your head on straight
You may lose him forever
When he walks out that gate

Some day you'll plead and beg
And it'll do no good to cry
You've showed him the door before
This time maybe goodbye

Think before you do it
Think who is to blame
He may have had enough
And he's onto your game

Remember the good in him
Remember the positives
Remember the good times
And the love that he gives

You know he's been good to you
And you know that he cares
So don't push him too far
He may heed your dares

Its a lonely life ahead
Till another one comes along
Think back to number one
Why everything went wrong

Hang onto your man
Check your attitude
Better straighten up your act
Before you lose this dude

SITTIN BY THE CAMPFIRE

Sittin here by the campfire
My mind begins to dream
I think of the 49ers
When their wagons crossed this stream

I wonder about their hardships
Wagons bursting at the seams
Cutting trails in the wilderness
And the crossing of the streams

From the prairie to the mountains
To the gold fields and the sea
To fulfill thier hopes and dreams
Wandering what life will be

I wander what was really
Going through their mind
Were they looking toward the future
Or loved ones they left behind

Looking over their shoulders
To keep their wagons safe
Keep on plodding forward
And always keep their faith

To endure all kinds of weather
The dust storms of the plains
Clouds roaring with thunder
Muddy trails from the rains

They were making histery
It hadn't crossed their minds
Just lookin toward the future
And the working of the mines.

RANCHER'S DAUGHTER

She was the ranchers daughter
The prettiest in the land
I worked for her father
The ranch was the bar x brand

I longed to get to know her
I knew that bye and bye
She was my inspiration
And I'd like to be her guy

We met out on the trail
I stopped to say hello
I was greeted with a smile
With eye's that seemed to glow

I'd always check my manners
Not to hurry her too much
Our meetings were always pleasant
We aimed to keep in touch

I finally got my courage
To ask her to dance
She threw her arm's around me
I knew I had a chance

Her father was on to us
He took me too the side
He raised my pay and said to me
It takes money to take a bride

I want you two to get married
And this is what he said
You've earned my daughter's love
I want you to run this spread

LIFE IN THE HIGH COUNTRY

To live in the high country
The place everyone should be
To stand on a mountain top
And believe how far you can see

To live half way up a mountain
You're half way in between
The garden's in the valley
And the mountain peak's so clean

Half way up the mountain
Rock garden's and pines
Beautiful scenery
And history of the mine's

Living in the mountain's
The folk's in mountain town's
Enjoy music and dancing
Whispering water fall sound's

To live in the high country
A place everyone should be
To stand on a mountain top
To believe how far you can see

RETIRED

I headed for the mountains
I had no bridges to burn
So never burn your bridges
They'll be there for your return

I headed for the mountain's
Set up camp on a mountain stream
I've made my home in the mountains
Fulfilled a life long dream

I headed for the mountain's
Had no bridges to burn
Never burn your bridges
They'll be there for your return

When I decend to the valley
I see the change in trend's
I see lot's of commotion but
It's nice to see my friends

I hurry back to my mountain home
I love the altitude
Back to the pine's and river
You'll know where to find this dude

I headed for the mountains
Had no bridges to burn
So never burn your bridges
They'll be there for your return

JUST THINKIN

I spend my time thinkin
If you think the same as me
You wonder whats on my mind
I want you on my knee

If you spend your time a thinkin
And you think the same as me
I think you gave me a clue
You want to be on my knee

Lets put our minds together
We'll be a perfect team
Lets you and I get married
And we'll persue our dream

We can do what we want
Be what we want to be
I want to be your lover
So will you marry me

LEAVE MY GIRL ALONE

I know that you're a roudy bunch
And I don't like your tone
You'll have to answer to me
Just leave my girl alone

I could see the danger
As they tried to stare me down
I turned my back to walk away
They pinned me to the ground

I bowed my back and kicked my feet
And I'm really gettin mad
Grabbed a leg and collar
And gave it all I had

I broke one arm and tore a shirt
That cut them down to three
I got up stomping mad
And kicked one in the knee

One was just a little squirt
But he thought he was tough
Thats the one I tore his shirt
Thats when I got rough

I threw him into another punk
The one with the broken arm
If you give me any more lip
You'll buy the farm

Now get your rear ends outa here
And if you'd like another whirl
I'll take you apart from limb to limb
If you ever bother my girl

ODE TO BY FRIEND'S

The American Indian walks softly and slow
He is ever so gentle and talks very low
Thinks deeply of what he says
He knows where he wants to go

His feelings have been hurt
And his pride taken away
Cause the white man took over
To destruct as they may

The Indian was courageous
In their unending plight
Bow and arrow against powder
In a lop-sided fight

We insulted him deeply
Left him in despair
Neglecting to give him
The right to clear the air

We took his land
His only tool
He wants it back
We call him a fool

We capitalize on his history
And I wonder if it's fair
There seems to be a mystery
Why we were even there

The Indian must be thinking
How selfish we must be
To take his heritage
And peddle it with glee

101

I MAY LOOK LIKE A COWPOKE

When you see me in the city
You never know for sure
I may look like a cowpoke
But my boots show no manure

I won't be wearing a gun belt
On my shoulder you won't find a chip
I may look like a cowpoke
But no pearl handle's to grip

I wear a bolo and a western hat
Decked out in western shirt and jean's
You may think I'm a cowpoke
Cause there are no in betweens

My western boot's aren't pointed
And a horse I've never sat
I couldn't find the stirrup
A saddle don't fit my pratt

I'm just a plain ole mountain man
I love my western life
Hiking trails and a mountain stream
And sharing with my wife

When you see me in the city
You never know for sure
I may look like a cowpoke
But my boots show no manure

NOT ONE FOR TROUBLE

I rode into town one day
And stopped to have a beer
I side stepped a cowpoke
Sliding out on his rear

Now I'm not one for trouble
Just need sometime to think
The hombre that hit the cowpoke
Had too much to drink

He straddled up beside me
Just a little to my right
I could see the look in his eye
This hombre wants to fight

He got loud and ugly
I'm trying to keep my cool
He grabbed me by the arm
I knock him off the stool

Up he comes for another round
as I turned on my seat
He took around house pass at me
I knocked him off his feet

Now I'm just a friendly guy
And I don't know your name
But if you taunt me any more
I'll give you more of the same

A BIT OF HISTORY

White man Invaded the Indians
Relentlessly drove them back
Called savage for protecting
Over powered by white man flack

We took their land
And showed our greed
We called them redskins
Or half breed

And to this day
We help other countries
And don't make them pay

We help our minority
The American way
Indians aren't priority
And we say nay

They show us charm
And cause us no pain
They lost the farm
And have nothing to gain

Our blacks have been cared for
Hispanics too
The chinese and boat people
Are given their due

We fail to admit
That our selfishness Is real
We have two sets of values
Neither one a big deal

The Indian was robbed
Of his pride and self esteem
We set up laws
And shattered their dream

We gave them arid property
And forced them to stay
We left them in poverty
The rest of their day

We didn't offer to share
In their loss of the land
White man didn't care
Wouldn't lend them a hand

It's time we pay homage
To who's country we took
And for the massacre
Theres been written a book

In my heart there is guilt
From which this country was built
Our two sets of values
Were pushed to the hilt

I visited Spearfish
In the northern black hills
Each reminder of Indians
Gave me cold chills

Their heritage is comercialized
And peddled with force
My dream is to finalize
The statue of Crazy Horse

Lets dig in our pockets
Come up with some dough
Lets give them the power
To get on with the show

Great white father
Lets show our esteem
So the American Indian
Can finish a dream

49'er Trail

Yesteryear Is full of history
As we think of the wagon trains
Crossing the rugged mountains
After months across the plains

The hardships were plenty
20 miles was a very good day
To cross the mountains before winter
They had to leave in may\

From St Louis to Ogallala
They trod across the plains
Challenging mother nature
First the sand storms,then the rains

They had to grease the axles
Keep the wagons going strong
And tend to the live stock
most anything could go wrong

It,s all up hill to Laramy
The horses will need some rest
It's only the beginning
It's a long ways to the west

Across Wyoming to the Great Salt Lake
Will take another six weeks
Up and down and around
To circle the mountain peaks

The scouts will find a water hole
Check out a place to rest
A hard day in the blazing sun
Puts every one through the test

It's been a long way
Since a town of any size
All you see in the distance
Is where the mountains meet the skies
You wander if you'll ever get there
As you study a western peak
It seems so close but oh so far
To get there in a week

When you finaly get there
You're amazed at what you see
Theres always another mountain
How many more, how can it be

Lo and behold, another world opens up
We're approaching the Great Salt Lake
Two days away and all down hill
Its time for another break

Dip the dipper in the bucket
When ever you want a drink
They didn't have faucets or showers
Didn't even have a sink

No one ever complained
Not even a sound
About getting out the blankets
And sleeping on the ground

Every one up for breakfast
At the first light of day
Pack all the gear in the wagons
Soon they're on their way

Six more weeks across the desert
The sierra's come in sight
One more pass to over come
To add to their awesome plight

Late May to September
All summer they carried on
The biggest task before them
Top old Donner summit, to the gold fields beyond

From Truckee Meadows to the summit
Should take about a week
Can you imagine the celebration
As they pass old Donner peak

Of all their wildest dreams and hope
The last of their dream comes true
As they clammered down the western slope
To start their life anew.

A storm a brewing

There's a storm a brewing
I can feel it in my vains
There's a storm a brewing
I can tell before it rains

When every one gets moody
Everything seems so still
There's a storm a brewing
The moment seems to chill

It's time to collect our feelings
I can feel it in my vains
Perspective is the answer
I can tell before it rains

When there's a storm a brewing
Lets try to hold our head
Put it in perspective
Before too much is said

When everybody's riled
The wind begins to blow
There's a storm a brewing
I'll tell you why I know

There's a storm a brewing
I can feel it in my vains
There's a storm a brewing
I can tell before it rains

Till after I was gone

I'm tired moving in and out
Things will never be the same
You get a nasty attitude
And stick me with the blame

Got a chip on your shoulder
And it really makes me sad
With all your accusations
Makes me look so bad

My clothes were on the door step
I disappeared before the dawn
You never knew you loved me
Till after I was gone

You finally reconsidered
But the battle lines were drawn
You didn't know you loved be
Till after I was gone

Cheer up

It's hard to see the sunshine
While holding back the tears
It's hard to hide your feelings
Through everyone else's cheers

You see the plastic allusions
That penetrate your fears
Your reasons are just confusions
That nobody hears

Your mind is a churning maze
Obtacles from every angle
Opposites of every phase
Your nerves begin to jangle

Your reasons are inferior
Disenters shatter your thinking
The harder you try the worst it gets
Your spirit is slowly sinking

Your friends are few and far between
As you drift into your shell
The lowest moment you could dream
A life of living hell

No response to hear the hell
Your pride is gone forever
There's no roses for to smell
You've lost your last endeavor

Shut down your mind
Stop blaming yourself and natch
Troubles will come to a grind
Then you can start from scratch

The world around us is beautiful
Shed the tears and look
Chase away the goblins
Write a different book

Start it out with a happy smile
Forget the frowns and sneers
Be good to yourself for a while
Your heart will throb of cheers

Lighten your load, remove the weight
Take sometime and rest your soul
Then you'll find its not too late
Your spirit is on a roll

To love yourself and
Keep your pride
Be good to yourself
All your troubles will hide

You'll grow and acquaint yourself
With a person you've never known
Your dreams will enhance your spirit
A star that has always shown

Smell the roses, study the trees
You'll find the sunshine, enjoy the breeze
Put your sights on the future
Your heart will be at ease

Now you're up and on your feet
Your world is easier to bare
You're on the right track
I know, cause I've been there

HAPPY DAYS

Happy days are here again
Everything's looking up
Things are easy and fall in place
Your spirit is a buttercup

Now don't make all those promises
Don't get yourself too deep
Find sometime for leisure
Or back you'll slowly creep

Let your heart go seeking
Give it lots of space
Your charm begins to show
In the smile about your face

Don't worry about others problems
Let them solve their own
Enlighten them with a smile
They'll see how you have grown

Ease their mind with friendliness
Don't greet them with a frown
Sometimes a friendly gesture
Will lift them when they're down

Have happy thoughts and be merry
To everyone you see
They'll see the warmth you carry
Just like they'd like to be

When they see you nonchalant
They still know that you care
Just because you smile a lot
Shows that you're aware

121

To Stay A Friend

When we get acquainted
It seems to be so nice
We prowl and investigate
And add a little spice

We should mix it up
But not too good
Leave a little flavor
Leave it at that, we should

Cause when we mix it up too good
It can get overdone
Takes away the imagination
And spoils all the fun

When we quit wandering
The magic will be gone
No mysteries for pondering
And we'll begin to yawn

For when we can't imagine
No secrets left to tell
We take away the mysteries
No excitement left to quell

Let's keep our juices flowing
And don't rock the boat too much
Our secrets won't be showing
We won't be out of touch

When we get to know each other
Our attitudes will change
Our differences will collide
Our feelings will be strange

123

Our memories will be saddened
Our wishes unfulfilled
Our feelings will be maddened
Our love will be chilled

To start another friendship
Will be a cautious move
Be careful how we do it
Stay out of that hostile groove

The Loss Of A Friend

To lose a friend for petty reasons
Is a strikeout at best
We both have dIfferent visions
But we have the same request

The paths we crossed were mean't for us
We shared in all our thoughts
Our values got tangled up
Tied our nerves into knots

Our universe was complicated
Our emotions over flowed
Our nuanses were over rated
A friendship we couldn't hold

Our paths are long and lonely
Our feelings are hurt and cold
The scars will always be there
As if they had been scrolled

There's an open circuit in our visions
Why it happened we don't really know
And a short in our feelings
I find it hard to let you go

Our love turned to turmoil
Our friendliness to friction
Our feelings insecure
Our tenderness to restriction

WE lost our understanding
And a closeness that was real
Our hearts were too demanding
To a wound that wouldn't heal

I know it's hard for me
And the same is true for you
But lets be friends again
It doesn't have to be so blue

It is said that time will heal
A heart that is shaken
But the damage is for real
And the reasons are forsaken

Lets try to remember the good times
And let the blues go by
Show our true feelings
The ones we cant deny

We'll continue our journey
And learn to cope with pride
Although there will be feelings
Impossible to hide

Patience

You always are complaining
I don't seem to make the grade
I know that things are tight
Just trying to learn a trade

You're never there to greet me
When I come through the door
You always seem disgusted
Don't seem to love me any more

It sure would be nice to hear
A compliment or two
Or just a friendly smile
But you're always in a stew

Go back to your mother
Tell her how bad I am
Tell her how bad it is
How your life is in a sham

Your mother knows how hard I work
And she knows my love for you
She can read between the lines
By the picture that you drew

Mother said to go back home
Let him learn his trade
Show some love and patience
Get off of this charade

He'll make a good living
Takes good care of the yard
You should be grateful
Don't lean on him so hard

NowI've learned my trade
And the moneys rolling in
Things are looking up
It's nice to see your grin

'Now that things are easier
we're as happy as can be
As we begin to show our love
Me for you and you for me

OUR LORD OUR HEAVEN

My lord is the same as yours
We see him in different ways
He's forever in our presence
We thank him for his praise

My heaven is also yours
It's not so far away
Our gift of life and feelings
Our belief should never sway

Heaven is not out of reach
The comfort that we feel
The answers to our prayers
To hear us when we kneel

When we feel alone
His presence filters in
He lifts up our spirits
When our mood is wearing thin

Be positive and keep our faith
We will be alright
Show love and compassion
Help others see the light
To believe in the lord
Pray that he will hear it
He is always with us
There is no need to fear it

Close your eyes and speak to him
You'll feel his warmth and love
His hand will touch your spirit
Feel the blessing from above

I thank my lord for being there
To carry me in his palm
Protect me when there's trouble
To guide and keep me calm

Sometimes we wonder where you are
While waiting for some clues
But you blessed me with patience
That's how we pay our dues

We know that you are busy
When we ask you for your blessing
When we think you didn't hear us
We were only reminessing

While looking after others
We'll try to help you too
Extend a hand and show our love
The warmth that comes thru you
Amen